ANNA WOODFORD
Everything is Present

SALT

CROMER

PUBLISHED BY SALT PUBLISHING 2025

2 4 6 8 10 9 7 5 3 1

First published in Great Britain in 2025 by
Salt Publishing Ltd
12 Norwich Road, Cromer, Norfolk NR27 0AX, United Kingdom

GPSR representative
Matt Parsons matt.parsons@upi2mbooks.hr
UPI-2M PLUS d.o.o., Medulićeva 20, 10000 Zagreb, Croatia

www.saltpublishing.com

Salt Publishing Limited Reg. No. 5293401

A CIP catalogue record for this book is available from the British Library

ISBN 978 1 78463 350 9 (Paperback edition)

Typeset in Sabon by Salt Publishing

Printed and bound in Great Britain by Clays Ltd, Elcograf S.p.A

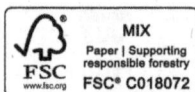

For all my kind mothers (most especially, Moira)

Contents

Everything is Present

End

Portrait of My Grandparents as Souvenirs

Granddad is holding a lucky Polish penny.
Granny has a pig's head on a breadboard.
Granddad is praying though his Torah is
upside down. Granny is playing the fiddle.
Granddad's insides have been hollowed out
of wood and he has a slot in his back.
Granny is squishy plasticine. Behind this beard,
Granddad is hiding. Behind this candle, Granny
burns for their son who is nowhere to be seen
in these tourist traps around the old ghetto –
he escaped to Nottingham and got a job at Raleigh.
Now he is a silver bicycle on my charm bracelet
or a tiny house, for the terrace
he named Lwów after the home he lost.

'Zydki' or 'Lucky Jew' figures are sold throughout Poland.

Easing

May 2020

Now the living room is a garden, there are flowers
in its living rug and cats buried at a far frayed edge.
Dad is muffled, despite the weather. All the flags
in Mum's face are warning, without walls
to whisper behind about his worsening.
Idols shouldered from the High Church
Of My Childhood, my parents perch on flimsy chairs.
No-one comes close to them. For want of a hug,
I am talking, talking, talking. I just want to hold them
before they disappear. In a corner, a bright ball
conjures my son and Mum when she could run
around after him. Nothing is lost in the long grass.

Go, Mum!

And then, at the end of your life – of our life
together – the walls of the hospital cracked,
the roof fell in. There were doors in ceilings,
in mattresses, in trolleys. Everywhere was an exit.
You were getting away. Sister called and I ran
like I was trapped in a Sharon Olds poem –
and yes, I knew the near body on the side ward spied
out of the side of my eye was you, even as I ran past,
even as the porter gestured back. I knew as you knew
when I burst in through the door as if through the wall
(your superhero). The ward was a rose garden,
a box in a theatre, a shopping centre – anywhere
we had had all our adventures. Heads together,
we bounced on the bed (you were getting higher
and higher). Your hand, which would no more
have not squeezed mine than fly, did not squeeze mine.
You were flying, Mum. Bloody Great Death
was at every window, jemmying them open
so you could make clean away in your hospital gown
with your skirt full of scrumped apples – the Dad apple,
the yoga apple, the Dr John apple, the Anna apple
polished and balanced on top. Before anyone
could come running with another care plan, another scan,
some *Warfarin*, you were leaving – your body open-mouthed
at its own agonal breathing. What could I do
but cheer you on – Go Mum! Go for it! Moira, Go!

Bright Side

I was expecting grief
to be that childhood dream without
the waking up part, to her singing
coming from the kitchen. I was not ready
for the sparkly colours of all
the other mothers as they swung
down from the ceiling, stepped through
the house's blasted side, sprang
out of doorways like Uma Thurman
in *Kill Bill* but holding Himalayan
salt lamps and chocolate care packages.
I was not expecting to be grabbed
mid-sentence about how well I was
doing *Come Here* and taken in
for a hug, for all the naughty
lockdown hugs to feel like safe
sex, for my body to be open
as a fresher's to any passing stranger's,
for how everything was suddenly
a sign – the sign in the chemist's *Own
Your Own Skin* the subway graffiti
Be Nice Man then Christmas,
that old tree, to be brought out
and not be too shabby. I was not expecting
my father to fall from out of my mother's
sleeve, for him to career on his castors
in the middle of a clapping circle
and for the wheel not to come off –
I think of Compo in *Last of the
Summer Wine* going gloriously

downhill in a cut loose side-car
to a honking great soundtrack set against
an area of outstanding natural beauty.
I was not prepared for the fun we had finally
after forty odd years. *Well, that's a fine thing*
I can hear Mum saying in mock indignation
revelling as ever for ever and ever in everything
and anything that brings me pleasure.

FYI

My mother did not send you a rainbow.
I know that she loved me. I have no need
for Himalayan bath soak or a candle to conjure
warm, special memories. It's not time that heals but
that healing takes time is PTO scribbled on both sides
of a *Post-it*. 'Where else would I be?' Mum mutters
when someone says she is always with me,
reacting to news of her death the way she advised
if anyone said I looked tired – 'Really? No, not at all.
Someone was only just saying how well I looked.'

I Was Never Subtle

Head and shoulders above the *gîtes*
and flowers, how she sent herself up
for my disposable camera, fanning
her full many-coloured skirt in both hands
and gathering into its showy folds, the Alps,
the purity of the water, the toppermost
chapel cum goat shed (not Notre-Dame
could compete). What was it she said
when the photos came back in their bright
envelope that September? Ah, I remember

all year how she gobbled the *A Vous
La France!* language cassettes until at last
the macarons, the madames, the afternoon's
'siesta' with Dad while we kids peeled off
our skin. That was when my mother
was a woman. Now she is a rainbow above
Holy Island on the first day of the first year
without her – not a wishy washy one – so solid
even I who am over rainbows start to lift
my phone to the heavens with all the other trippers.

The Freeman

September 2021

I could speak to the doctors, the nurses, the physio.
I could speak to the wall. I could phone again
between 2 and 3 or later. I should only worry
if I got a call. I could speak to her until
she couldn't pick up then my calls went
to Dad's coat pocket. I could buy nighties.
I could bag Munros at weekends ready to lay
at her slippered feet like potatoes. I could beg
all I pleased. The government were everywhere.

I could go in. Someone waved open every closed door –
    it was her all over   using   her dying   breath trying
to find another another   breath   to give me –
Someone told me she could hear then withdrew their head.
It's not the end of the world she would have said.

Portrait of My Grandfather as The Kennewick Man

My grandfather is about 9,300 years old.
　　His crania rests outside
of any modern group, on the soft banks
　　of the River Trent. His greatcoat is open
around his bones which cedar boughs have protected
　　from coyote (only the femurs are missing).
He ate salmon and there were small tins
　　of low-fat beans in his net-
bag, after widowhood then diabetes.
His worn molars will not yield
reliable measurements but he speaks to me
　　in the five languages Gran said
he knew, in the words Leopolis Lwów Lviv
and in the echo of my father's stammer.
　　His skeleton carries such weight it cannot lie.

I am digging up the sacred ground of my childhood
　　garden, using my fingers and what is left of the family
silver – beside me is a Stork SB tub
　　of medals, blurred photos and the memories
my grandfather stuffed in his pockets. Behind me
　　my brother and father, mother and sister
are waving clap-sticks and shaker-bells
　　in this poem which is an elevated canoe
for my grandfather – who was displaced – to take him back
　　before sundown to the Happy Hunting Grounds.

The Kennewick Man was the name given to the remains of a prehistoric
man found in Kennewick, USA in 1996. The discovery led to controversy
between the Umatilla people who wanted the skeleton returned to them and
archaeologists who wanted the remains to be displayed in a museum. The
Kennewick Man was exhibited for over a decade before being reburied in 2017.

Delirium (Great Balls of Fire)

Freddie Fingers Lee's hat is on fire,
he has poured petrol into its inner tube
and is playing the piano blindfolded above
Dad's boarded-up fireplace. A firefighter
is fitting a smoke alarm that will fall
an hour after she has gone. In twenty-four hours,
Dad will be lying dehydrated under a picture
of Derwentwater, wanting the hospital to keep him in.
For now, he is unsteady in the living room Mum's Death
has whipped through, refusing medication, a stick, care.

Dad was friends with Tongue-Tied, Rocking Jimmy,
Freddie Fingers when he lived in County Durham,
next to a woman whose horse had free rein
of the kitchen. Dad got called The Doc. The doctor,
hauling him up by the armpits, calls him *lad*.
The triage nurse *my lovely* when he can't tell her
what year it is. It is 13 January 2004,

the year of Griff Steel and the Duck and Dive Five,
Dad writes in 'Now Dig This'. It is 1962, Jerry Lee Lewis
has just set fire to a reporter's face and shaken
Dad's hand outside Newcastle City Hall. It is sometime
in my childhood, Linda Gail (Jerry's sister) is on the phone
to Mum, telling her she has been married seven times
because she doesn't believe in fornication, telling her
she will have Van Morrison's balls. (By then Linda has already
composed the song whose words will appear on Mum's gravestone.)

What is the point of remembering today with its endless grief,
its queue of people asking you what day it is and if you know
where you are. Its pulled cubicle curtains, its social workers
called Jeff, its stairs tests and its unsatisfactory
snacks. Dad would pour a coke bottle full of gasoline
over today and set light to it. *I had no favourites,*
I hated you all equally, he cracks when he is admitted
to Ward 20. *Beat that, Chuck!* I can hear The Killer
cackle, playing on, and on and on, on his burning piano.

'The Former Life.'

Gran wrote on an envelope
seventy odd years ago
in her infant teacher's hand.

A4 windowless manila,
not enough space on its surface
for a man to plant both his feet on.

Not enough space inside
for a childhood to breathe.
'The Former Life' Full Stop

A contract between them. Kept
in the outhouse with the out of reach bottles,
spidery potatoes, damaged packets

that fell from the line. *He took
what work he could get* Dad said
though on 5 day of March 1939

John Casmir University certified him
as a Master of Law. Here he is, all
eyes, in a displaced persons' camp.

Here is a faded book of Thirteen
Polish Legends. In 1947, he changed
his name to Richard, leaving behind

this old stuff that can never
be sorted out, for others to hang on to,
to hold up to the light.

After You

I want to run home with today with its big yellow sun,
its blue, the sky-blue of a netball top, and show you
my A++ in grieving. I want to nail being a Mum
the way you did, with your red shiny nails
you got painted at Beauty Spot and your knitted beanie.
How you saluted the sun every morning
and if you saw a top you liked, bought it
three times then gave them away. The way you had
Maureen and Terry and wine is the way I have
Helen and Kirsty and wine. A year after you died,
how I love bumping into you on Gosforth High Street
with your overflowing bags and your sparkly
pom-poms shouting *Go Anna! Go Anna! Go!*

Middle

Grabber

I have seen it done. The swinging metal claw
drop onto the plush white bunny, raising it above
the rolled wads of cash, digital watches and grubby
Sindies – wobble but
       hold   hold   hold
until hovering over the lit-up chute,
with much fanfare, let go
of its little target. Mike opened the hatch
and pulled out the rabbit
for me to cuddle, make much of and call Charlotte.

Maybe it was in another century. Maybe it was
before the machines were rigged. Maybe
men shouldering big cats and teddies
through fairgrounds *are* being paid
but Mike himself, my first boyfriend,
was a soft white bunny – like my period,
like uni, like all the things I thought would never
come. Now I am married (bunny), a mother (bunny),
have a blue door, a black cat, a working life (bunny bunny bunny)
and am struggling to pick up to hold onto cuddlywarmandfluffy
among all the highly flammable shit, as a monk holds peace
by training the fingers of his mind. I have never seen it
done again (drop it!) but I have seen it done (hang on!).

Seeing Joe

There was a corridor I had to grow inside me
leading to a room where I had to learn to be still.

Your phone was on divert. Your practice was an extension
of your home with no polished receptionist or sign.

Every week, every fortnight, every month eventually
we talked while the elephant in the room

clambered onto the table, shook its hips, shat
over everything until I wanted to scream and jump about

like the Blue Peter presenter from years ago
with his hurty elephant-trodden-on foot.

You had no time for years ago. We went there once
and didn't linger. You blew a raspberry

at pills, support groups, other counsellors
They are all called things like Caroline Lingard.

Your everyday suburb was new to me. Now I know
where the 7 bus goes. On my last visit,

you gave me an apple from your plentiful tree -
it was raining apples that year with its crazy weather.

LotsofPeopleinaRoom

I have no answers but how I love
lotsofpeopleinaroom and me coming in
as the teacher especially when my life
is one big question or even two
or three people and the librarian,
the community worker, the volunteers
with their telltale lanyards filling in
for actual people, making a dent
in my stack of handouts. How I love
the urn, the hour of it, being introduced
as Anna Woodfield, the woman with rhubarb
sticking out her bag, the man who whispers
he has had to learn to speak again
and, lining the way, the kids outside
the vape shop giving me directions
when I don't know where I'm going;
the passengers on the wobbly train
to Sowerby Bridge or Sandal
who have held my hand unknowingly;
the would-be passengers where trains
don't go, watching ghost buses appear
and disappear on the screens. How I love
the casual love, duck or darling,
love someone's granny in a café
making me poached eggs when I am far
from home and love when I am back
home, feeling like myself again, just
hanging with the downward dogs
in yoga. How I love a handful
of people but love my neighbour more

some days, so much I would keep her
talking. Let me let her in when she comes
knocking at my door. Let me remember
all she brings is sugar sugar sugar.

Derailed

Twenty years ago, how one minute we were
on a train going places a year after uni and
the next minute we were holding each other
waiting to die and the next minute we were
holding each other waiting to die and then
how ridiculous we were suddenly hanging around
waiting in our no longer solid carriage. HelenandI
wrappedaroundeachother like a couple of Klimt's
women on a curling student poster. When we knew
we weren't going to roll over, the thought flew
into my head wearing Wonder Woman pants
and a push up bra *This is your chance to be a hero!*
Then the girl appeared – my-girl-tied-to-a-train-track
but little and crying for her mother. I held her
until the man took her from me and passed her
through the smashed window, leaving the little girl
inside of me wanting to hang on to her still.

Back on solid ground, for years after we laughed
about the mother locked in the loo, about the man
who sat on Helen's suitcase and burst it though
it had survived a train crash, about the shit Indie band
in the next carriage who strummed while we waited
for taxis and I forgot – or forgot to remember enough -
the smashed glass, the wanting to be first out,
even the little girl until she came clambering in
through this afternoon's window (in through the poem-
door that is always chocked). Now she wanders
across my desk's fallout of papers, writing off
whatever I was writing for this. I don't want to get all heavy

about a prang, a comedy shunt from a runaway digger,
a kick up the arse from a wrathful Buddha. Still I am in awe
of how we nearly died twenty years ago and knew
to just hold each other, then the lightness with which
we scrambled up the bank and back into our lives.

Women as Tables

after 'This Girl Bends' by Kerry Stewart (1996)

Not Allen Jones' spike-heeled mannequin,
down on all fours on a bit of sixties
spread sheepskin, with a table top
bolted to her back and bare breasts
screaming *Knave*, nibbles, cocktail sausages

but her flat-footed kid sister, scrubbed face
facing upwards. She proffers the board
of her chest and torso. Her arms are fused
to her sides. She looks unstable –
if she is a table at all, she is not
for the faint-stomached. Her housecoat
is the colour of flesh that has been
dredged from a river. *Touch me* she says
and you'll be wearing your dinner.

2020

Since all of this and the sun, I have fallen
in love with you again – taking me back
to the bubble of your flat with its solid
teapot which was the very beginning of our family
home, the bowls – all chipped now,
that rug you bought in Kerala or wherever
you had been all my life. I think of your spoons
with their dear open faces, your knives
with no sharp edges and, especially, the warm dark
of your bedroom like the insides of an airing cupboard
where a child might giggle during a game of Sardines.
Now I know I will be with you and our son
at the end of the world – here
in our own back yard with its little shout of colour.

Evening Prayers

The way the monk prostrates
in front of all-comers

flat out in his lit robes,
revealing his maroon socks

are threadbare, is all I need
to know of sex. I don't know

where to look. My hands are awkwardly
shaped into a begging bowl on my lap.

The door to this room is wide open –
anyone can tip up off the street.

Beginning

Pyjama Jump

A bit buttoned up for all my near nakedness,
frolicking on the steps of the university's closed offices –
less a *silly slag*, as Simon said, and more
one of the bare bottomed cherubs playing
among the dandelion clocks in my childhood
bedroom, despite the spiders in that old picture's
border with their many leggy Simon eyes.

Such a night! Snogging Everyone! Everyone's
Boyfriend! The night got banned just after
we graduated (by then we were wise
to its sadness). Still, I would embrace
my would-be wantonness – briefly
holding everyone dear and kissing
and kissing and kissing. Regardless.

Pyjama Jump was a messy event in the Sheffield student calendar where
participants took part in a pub crawl cross-dressed in nightwear in November.

Coming,

after months of struggling
to find the right words
to keep the wrong love
from leaving – getting
down like Rumpelstiltskin's
princess to the last ugly
possibilities   *Sheepshank*
Laceleg   then
I Won't   *I Promise*
I'llDoAnything   only for him
to turn tail anyway –

your whispered *Baby*
at the base of my spine
was balm butter
kiss it better

as if it was the first time
I'd heard it as if
you happened
upon a password
magicking a door
that had never appeared
in the dark with other men

– less a door
    more a ribbon curtain –

into a room filled with,
for jewels and riches,
just your dressing gown
and slippers and you
with your sword in your hand
and there were no dragons.

I have to go out half ready, badly made
up, so one day I will be ready properly.
It will take years. I have leggings for a hairband
and Mum's tights on and a little skirt to undercut
my big boots (my childhood is a scrap
of toilet paper stuck to one heel). I have *Juicy Fruit*,
concealer, a towel as well as a tampon
and am tossing my hair through the *Timotei* field
on my way to the bus-stop. One honk from a wound-
down car window and the metaphorical tray
I am carrying will clatter. Now I can marry, drive
a moped, have sex, leave school – I am going back
to school after two years at home in front of an artificial fire.
I have the password (16!) to the office of Newcastle
Careers Guidance. Newcastle is Annacastle upon Tyne.
It Is Time chimes the golden girl in the nip on Northern
Goldsmiths clock. Newcastle is the paved path
to London, to Liverpool, to Literature, Life and Thought.
For now, Newcastle is Newcastle College and The Broken Doll.
Mum keeps the door to the city on the sneck at night
and goes to snuggle in with Dad. Leave! says the door,
Come back with a love-bite, L-plates, a portfolio of your own
making or be an adult left behind in a childhood
bedroom, crushed like a martyr under the weight
of old trophies and Garfields. I need to rise out of my pit
like the Iron Man and get my clank on. I need to stop
hanging around. Already the circus of my adolescence
is being disbanded, its tigers and one trick ponies set free.
Next year, there will be flatmates, *Femidoms*, eighths
for breakfast, Nirvana will be everywhere and Rich
will be rattling my bedroom window with pebbles.

Room

John William Waterhouse muses kept coming unstuck.
James Dean covered up a damp patch. Photos of my brother
and his friends with their arms around me were casually
spaced. The house phone squatted by the door,
sometimes it tail got pulled out at the hall socket
and I carried on and on talking about Him before realising.
Above was The Messy Relationship – its mess seeping
into the communal areas, causing the cleaner to leave
a note. Below was where He slept and I lay on top dreaming
until the night He woke me up throwing her voice in the air
like juggling balls. We were down a ginnel, playing House
of Pain, Blur and REM, playing the scoring league
(1 for a snog, 2 for a snog and a – etc) thongs
coo-cooing on radiators and no toilet paper.
By the summer, we were slagging each other off
in the phonebox outside Happy Shopper and taking baths
at the landlady's if we wanted hot water. Mike and I
were riding around on my bedroom's white charger,
its hooves tit-tatting on His ceiling. If Mike wasn't there
to hold my hand, I hurried upstairs with my Tuna Frittata
on His plate, to wallow in that tacky room cum life
I couldn't fit a foot in now – not a big toe.

The Car Crash Of Our Relationship

Now a shelter for rough sleepers, badgers, magical creatures
under a protected Northumberland dark sky. For so long,
just a car crash. That girl, whose head I found on my pillow,
a week after we split. You walking away, unharmed.
You were not unharmed, I realised running into you
years later, it was just I was obsessed with the wreckage,
with one for the road in your big brass bed – Dylan
and Zeppelin, above – underneath, your treasure chest:
remember showing me *Songs of Innocence and Experience*,
the 'ping test' on your handful of gold coins?
Remember driving very slowly the long way round while I knelt
in the footwell, open-mouthed? It was another lifetime
before we had to pick our kids up from somewhere.

Coiners Country

In my childhood, that graveyard
was the haunt of the long-buried
King of the Coiners. He hung
over me in the chilly church-porch
where I stamped my boots
with my brother and sister, drying off
enough to get wet again.
On a bad day, it brightened up
and Dad hiked for miles – dragging us
past the rusted village-pump
that conjured prisoners' parched mouths
at the wall's barred hole, then past
the more and more solitary cottages
I wanted to be inside. Soon
we were sucking pebbles for water;
and adding them to the stony piles
marking the track to Coiners Country.

We were there when we reached the ruin
where the King had forged his coins'
clipped suns; then it was time
to turn back. The walk's highlight
was a burnt-out ice-cream van,
hovering like an ice-cream in the desert
of the Calder Valley. Over the hill
was a hypermarket, Dad promised
when hooves rattled in the air
around us. It was before planes
or sex – the long summer holiday
Mum stayed at home while we explored

the country without her. Years later
I discovered that graveyard's new field
and being seventeen. It was all
about posing for the camera then
with my arm around Plath.

Vision

Seeing Serena Keddy, who reeled
in assembly with each new trophy;
ringlets and her pumped feet flying
while the whole school clapped in time,

after decades, is like seeing
the kitschy Mary of a roadside shrine
wave suddenly across stopped
traffic. Gym ropes fall

like snakes from the sky's steel bar.
Father O' Neill booms Hosanna.
I cross to hear her message:
The girls are meeting in Carluccio's

then, haloed by the lights' changing,
she recites the old register's
rosary: *Joanne Asher, Joanne
Eskdale, Sally Dixon, Fiona Evans*

Her dancing girl is Calla Lilies,
Marigolds, Lady's Slippers at her feet.

Garage, 1988

Lingering in the most dangerous room of my childhood home
where racked tools cut the air and there are VOLTS
in a box on the wall is the sharp-smelling dark of 1988 –
that night I should have been dreaming of wars,
French verbs, the HighwayMan by Alfred Noyes,
the moon lighting my carpet of revision notes as I beat
Cara Simpson in my sleep – it was as if I was dreaming,
sat at the wheel of the family car, keeping Mum
guessing; her footsteps hot then cold in the far-off warmth
of the house, I was pretending to have run away from.

Notes on Kaye

If Kaye was a *Lego* figure, she would come with a set of *OEDs* in one hand and a menthol cigarette in the other and a little me, at 17, with an open book.

A funky furniture shop called *Kaye's Place* would have a warm brown table in its window, just cleared of the breakfast things.

Kayeday would be celebrated every Sunday for a couple of hours (reckoned up discreetly by Kaye). Everyone would wear their T-shirt sleeves rolled up, Kaye-style, and lots of lipstick and talk about Chaucer and put their five favourite heroines in order (and afterwards give the bill to their father).

Dad took Kaye's number from the noticeboard at work the way he took free tickets for shows at the amateur theatre but never went himself.

Kaye came after two years of my not going to school when university was suddenly back on the table. She was extra-curricular because the rest of the curriculum was just a college evening class where they taught us the wrong play.

Kaye had a cat called Juno who was evolving into a pouffe she said. Two women sitting together discussing literature is always hopeful she said.

Like the record player I used to spin my teddies on that wasn't a *Sodastream* and the portable typewriter that wasn't a *Shaker Maker*, Kaye wasn't a sociology teacher. (Dad's presents were rarely what was asked for but, in retrospect, cooler.) ↰

In the background, Kaye's man was a postmodern Ken who wore *Army & Navy* jumpers and knew things like whether there could be more than one protagonist.

In the margins of Stoppard, of Fitzgerald, of Mansfield is Kaye – her little asides buried in a box of revision in a left-behind bedroom.

As a castle creates a heath so outside of Kaye's house with its clambering clematis, Dad would sometimes be waiting – stopped a little (shy) of her house with his engine ticking over.

A Claim on the Estate of Miss Rene Shill

I would bring Coconut Pyramids, a *Dolmetsch* recorder, *Flowers
in the Attic* by Virginia Andrews, a hot pink *Tampax* holder
and lay them at the site of La Sagesse Convent High
by the lone building which summons Shill
rattling a tambourine, as if in front of the bulldozer.
Boys could wait at the gate. A slippery slope
led to the Dene and pregnancy and resits. Burglars,
who knew not what they did, stole our vinyl from A-S
but *We kept our Tchaikovsky, girls!* Magnificent Shill!
her mouth wide open as legs as she held on and on
to her top note. Maybe angels in indoor sandals
giggled on the roof of the nursing home as she broke
into a swan song in her wingback chair and shattered
the sad vase on the windowsill. We were fourteen,
vicious little metronomes. Overnight, we let her jokes
fall flat and laughed at the photo of her Carmen
which could have been anyone. Tone deaf, I was
a silent member of the choir. Still, hearing
of Shill's unsung death – I would raise my voice in middle age
to carry her to Arcady where the cherry blossoms blow.

Making sandcastles is like making love

Don't build a moat around it. Don't shy
from the tide or wind. Don't crumble
when bits start to crumble but
bring out your pretty shells whatever.
Let your body be blown along the dirty coast.
Fill your bucket. Gather ring-pulls and common
as muck jewels. Do it daily, doggedly;
a weathered jogger, an old hand with a metal
detector among the necking beach bodies.
His head bunts mine. The tip of his spade
slaps the wet sand. His face is a bright tug;
cherry cherry cherry in a row; a Christmas
dinner made of candy in the exposed
resort where sea-air fetched up childhood
illuminations, a rockpool's briny treasure,
my grandmother waving from a pier
as he went down on one knee. I would stay
in this place year after year over any far-flung
paradise. Our child cries out like seagulls
on the stairs for crisps or just because
the pc is lagging. A storm is brewing. Always
our bed is full of stuff but his touch
is a towel in every crevice, is being lifted
onto a small wall. Making sandcastles is
like making love. Making love is like making
poems. Don't build a moat around it. Don't shy.

Home/Time

How my son *is is is* five
minutes and four decades ago
was me. How he is now and ever
shall be on this golden afternoon
gathering conkers from an old tree.
How we stop look listen all the way
home home to Mum. How I carry him.

How Mum cannot open the door enough.
How she grabs our things as if against
a big lit clock. How her pinny is
all frills and no yoke, her fingers,
chocolate. How she drops
to her hunkers before my son
and send me to my room, to write this.

How *Tiny Tears* has chickenpox and *Grease*
is scratched. How the heart shaped hook
cries out for my poncho. How *Peppa Pig*
has got in and is stamping her boots
on the duvet. How Mum shushes my son
as they dance around me. How everything is
turning – *And How*! – at the window.

Acknowledgements

Bad Lilies, The Moth, The Poetry Review, Poetry Wales, The Rialto, Stand. The Forward Book of Poetry 2024 (Faber & Faber, 2023). *Beyond the Storm: Poems from the Covid 19 era* (Write Out Loud, 2021).

'Delirium (Great Balls of Fire)' won the Ledbury Prize in 2023.
'Portrait of My Grandparents as Souvenirs' won The Wigtown Prize in 2021.
'Go Mum!' was highly commended in the Forward Prize 2023 and in the Moth Poetry Prize, 2021.
'Home/Time' was commended in the Troubadour Poetry Competition 2024.
'*I Was Never Subtle*' was shortlisted in the Fish Poetry Prize 2022.
'16/17' was commended in the McLellan Poetry Prize 2019.
'2020' was displayed on the Tyne & Wear Metro system in a project for the Royal Literary Fund.
'Portrait of My Grandfather as the Kennwick Man' was written during a Leverhulme Fellowship at Durham Law School. I would like to thank Professor Tom Allen for his support.

Much of this book was written throughout two residences as a Royal Literary Fund Fellow at the School of English, Newcastle University and the Department of Nursing, Midwifery and Health at Northumbria University. Warm thanks to Steve Cook at the Royal Literary Fund and to my colleagues at Newcastle and Northumbria.

With thanks and love to my comrade.

Thanks and love also to Elizabeth Cook for her comments on a draft of the manuscript.

Love and thanks to Dad, Emma and Martin and, above all, to Geoff and Archie who make everything present.

This book has been typeset by
SALT PUBLISHING LIMITED
using Sabon, a font designed by Jan Tschichold
for the D. Stempel AG, Linotype and Monotype
Foundries. It has been manufactured using Holmen
Book Cream 65gsm paper, and printed and bound by
Clays Limited in Bungay, Suffolk, Great Britain.

CROMER
GREAT BRITAIN
MMXXV